FILET CROCHET

FOR CHURCHES

by
Rosemarie Peel

CONTENTS

© Rosemarie Peel 1993

ISBN 1 874688 03 6

Printed in England by
Printhaus Graphique Ltd
Northampton

First published in September 1993 by
Lacet Publications
29, St Nicolas Park Drive, Nuneaton, CV11 6DL

Introduction

The ecclesiastical patterns in this book have been designed to take full advantage of the easy techniques which filet crochet offers. The worker needs only a basic knowledge of crochet, then, by reading 'How to follow filet crochet charts' on page 5, all the different techniques will unfold.

Filet crochet is especially suitable for churches because its beauty can be seen from a distance. Careful use of the crochet will complement other embellishments such as flowers, carvings, sculptures and stained glass.

Every congregation is sure to have enthusiasts for this well known craft. Using the designs in this book, items can be made not only for the church but also for the church hall, the school, the home and bazaars. A bookmark or an edged cloth would be an appropriate gift for someone who is house-bound and no longer able to get to church.

Hopefully this book is filled with enough ideas to suit any church and to cover every place where this type of lace could be used.

So as not to waste time and effort, careful preparation is needed before starting to make a piece of crochet for a specific purpose. A number of points to be considered are listed below.

Before you start.....

* Discuss projects concerning the church with your priest, vicar or minister.
* Make sure you are familiar with the abbreviations (see page 4).
* Decide on the thread and appropriate hook (see page 6).
* Make one repeat of a chosen pattern and then calculate how many repeats will be needed for your measured area.
* Purchase enough thread (see page 7).

Abbreviations

STITCH	ABBREVIATION	SYMBOL
Chain	ch	⬯
Double crochet	dc	✕
Treble	tr	⟙

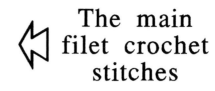

The main filet crochet stitches

Fasten off		►
Rejoin thread		▻

To fasten off cut the thread 15cm away from the crochet. Pull the loop on the hook until the cut end comes through. Put this end on a needle and oversew the fasten off point twice. Sew the end into the crochet for 3cm and trim only after the crochet has been blocked (see page 47).

When the pattern dictates, rejoin the thread by putting a slip-knot onto the hook and ss into the appropriate place.

Stitches for shaped edges and corners are:

STITCH	ABBREVIATION	SYMBOL	
Slip stitch	ss	⌒	
Double treble	dbltr	⟪	The dbltr and trtr are made in the usual way but are curved to fit into the pattern. The arrows show exactly where to place the hook when making the stitch. See the end of rows 2 and 3 in 'Sample pattern No.2' on page 9.
Triple treble	trtr	⟫	

Other abbreviations and symbols

The abbreviations and symbols shown above are standard ones used in crochet patterns worldwide.

Other abbreviations and symbols used in this book may not be standard so they are explained within the section they are used.

Left handers

Mirror image all the patterns. In written instructions change rights to lefts and vice versa and clockwise to anti clockwise etc.

How to read filet crochet charts

Filet crochet is generally worked in rows from side to side. The main stitches used are the chain, the double crochet and the treble (see Abbreviations on the opposite page).

These stitches are arranged in groups to form either a space, a block, a bar or a lacet. The arrangement of the stitches is shown below together with how they would be represented on a graph. On the square mesh of the graph a space is one empty mesh, a block is one filled mesh and a bar and lacet, when used together, cover a square of four meshes completed over two rows. The bar can also be used on its own, in which case it occupies two meshes in a row.

All the techniques used in this book are illustrated in the sample patterns (see pages 8/10).

	Stitches	As seen on a graph
A Space		
A Block		
A Bar and Lacet		

N.B. The last treble of a space, a block, a lacet or a bar is also the first treble of the next group. To illustrate this here are all four groups as they would be worked consecutively in a row.

TO START

Choose your thread and the appropriate hook (see page 7).
Make a slip-knot and put the loop on your hook.

CALCULATE THE CHAIN BASE

Look for the start line on the pattern.
Count the number of meshes required for the first row.
Multiply by 3 and add 1.
Add the appropriate number of turning chain for Row 1 (see page 6).
N.B. The loop on your hook is never counted.

FOLLOW THE ROWS

The starts of the rows in all patterns are numbered in order for one repeat of that pattern.
Be familiar with the sample pattern which relates to the pattern you have chosen to follow (see pages 8/10).

Handy tips

Put your hook under two loops when working onto trebles so as not to create ridges.

When working a lacet over a bar put the dc of the lacet over the 5ch of the bar. There is no need to use the middle ch.

There are three categories for working into chains:

1) At row ends work the last stitch into the appropriate chain stitch below, catching up two of its loops to give a firm edge.

2) When working a block over a space put the two middle tr of the block over the 2ch of the space. This does not alter the appearance of the crochet and is much quicker than working into each individual chain stitch.

3) Go into the actual chain stitch when making a foundation baseline either at the start or when increasing at row ends.

Turning chain

Instructions for all turning chain come at the end of the previous row. This is because it is neater and easier to make them before the work is turned. The length of the turning chain varies according to the first group of stitches on the next row.

A BLOCK has 3 turning chain to stand for the first tr of that block (e.g. Row 6, Sample pattern No.1 on page 8).

A SPACE has 5 turning chain to stand for a tr and 2ch (e.g. Row 2, Sample pattern No.1 on page 8).

A LACET has 6 turning chain to stand for the first tr and 3ch of that lacet (e.g. Row 4, Sample pattern No.1 on page 8).

A BAR has 8 turning chain to stand for a tr and 5ch (e.g. Row 5, Sample pattern No.1 on page 8).

INCREASING

6ch for one block increased at the beginning of the next row. Put the next tr of that block into the 5th ch from the hook. The next tr of this block will go into the first of the 6ch and the final tr will go into the last tr of the previous row.

8ch for one space increased at the beginning of the next row. Put the first tr of that row on top of the last tr of the previous row.

9ch for a two mesh increase where there is a block at the end of the row (e.g. Row 4, Sample pattern No.2 on page 9).

11ch for a two mesh increase where there is a space at the end of the row (e.g. Row 2 and Row 3 in Sample pattern No.2 on page 9).

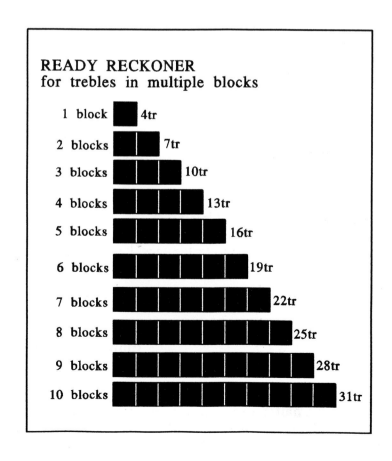

READY RECKONER
for trebles in multiple blocks

1 block	4tr
2 blocks	7tr
3 blocks	10tr
4 blocks	13tr
5 blocks	16tr
6 blocks	19tr
7 blocks	22tr
8 blocks	25tr
9 blocks	28tr
10 blocks	31tr

Hooks and thread

Always match your hook to the thread you intend to use. The table below shows the recommended pairings so that the finished work is neither too loopy nor too tight. The pairings can be altered slightly to suit the individual. For example the worker with tight tension would choose a size larger hook and the worker with slack tension would use a size smaller hook.

Available hook sizes	Hook comparison	Thread comparison	Some thread suggestions
0.50			
0.60	———	———————	A No.80 cotton such as DMC Fil a Dentelle
0.75			
1.00	———	———————	A No.40 cotton such as DMC Cordonnet
1.25	———	———————	A No.20 cotton such as Coats Opera
1.50			
1.75	———	———————	A No.10 cotton such as Lesur Empress
2.00			

Size guide ....approximate size of 22 meshes when worked in:

A No.80 cotton such as DMC Fil a Dentelle with a 0.60 hook

A No.40 cotton such as DMC Cordonnet with a 1.00 hook

A No.20 cotton such as Coats Opera with a 1.25 hook

A No.10 cotton such as Lesur Empress with a 1.75 hook

How much thread

With reference to the samples worked for this book, from the finest to the thickest threads:

One 5gm ball of DMC Fil a Dentelle No.80 is more than enough to work Bookmark I (see page 44).

One 20gm ball of DMC Cordonnet No.40 worked 10 repeats plus two corners of Edging XI (see page 26).

One 50gm ball of Coats Opera No.20 worked 'All corners' (see page 27).

One ball (400 yds) of Lesur Empress (equivalent to No.10 crochet cotton) works a small square curtain 50cm x 50cm such as the one illustrated on page 30.

It is better to buy too much thread than too little and, with the experience gained, use the excess on smaller items. The large piece of crochet (seven feet long by one foot deep) illustrated on page 33 used up 4 x 50gm balls of Coats Opera No.20. Unless you are going to attempt anything bigger then that would be an ample amount of thread for all large projects.

Sample pattern No.1
Filet crochet with straight edges

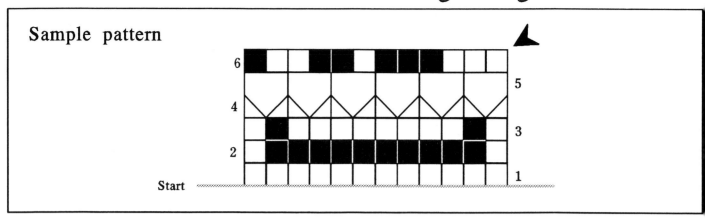

Sample pattern

The chart above is the pattern. The start line is shown together with the row numbers for the first repeat of the pattern.

To help the beginner follow this chart, details of all the stitches and complete written instructions are given below. Remember that, as the work is turned after each row, the work in your hand will only match the chart on alternate rows.

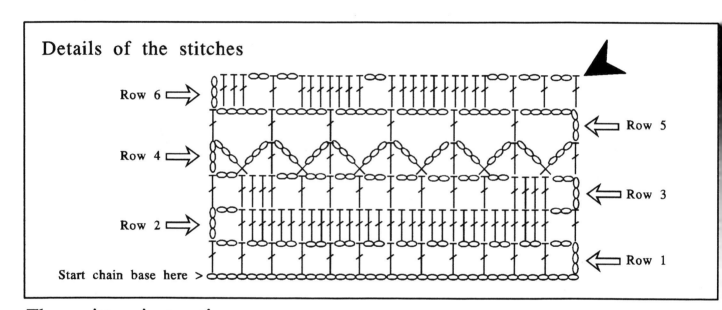

Details of the stitches

The written instructions

Refer to the abbreviations on page 4. If you are a beginner it would be a good idea to get someone to read these instructions for you while you follow the stitches on the illustration above.

To start make 42ch (37ch are the base line and 5ch are the turning ch for the first space of Row 1).

Row 1, 1tr into the 9th ch from the hook. (2ch, miss 2ch on the base line, 1tr into the next ch) 11 times, 5ch, turn.

Row 2, (1tr onto the next tr, 2tr over the next 2ch) 10 times, 1tr on the next tr, 2ch, 1tr into the 3rd of the 5 turning ch at the beginning of Row 1(catching up two loops of that ch), 5ch, turn.

Row 3, 4tr on the next 4tr, (2ch, miss 2tr, 1 tr on the next tr) 8 times, 3tr on the next 3tr, 2ch, 1tr into the 3rd of the 5 turning ch at the beginning of Row 2, 6ch, turn.

Row 4, 1dc on the next tr, 3ch miss 2tr, (1tr on the next tr, 3ch, 1dc on the next tr, 3ch) 5 times, 1tr into the 3rd of the 5 turning ch at the beginning of Row 3, 8ch, turn.

Row 5, (1tr on the next tr, 5ch) 5 times, 1tr into the 3rd of the 6 turning ch at the beginning of Row 4, 3ch, turn.

Row 6, 3tr over the next 3ch, 2ch, 1tr on the next tr, 2ch, miss 2ch, 3tr over the next 3ch, 1tr on the next tr, 3tr over the next 3ch, 2ch, 1tr on the next tr, 5tr over the next 5ch, 1tr on the next tr, 3tr over the next 3ch, 2ch, 1tr on the next tr, 2ch, 1tr over the middle of the 5ch bar, 2ch, 1tr into the 3rd of the 8 turning ch at the beginning of Row 5. Fasten off.

Sample pattern No.2
Filet crochet with shaped edges

Sample pattern

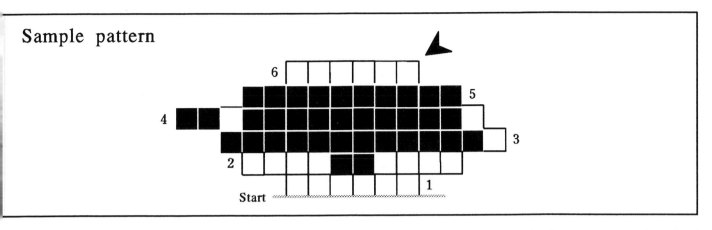

The chart above is for a pattern where increasing or decreasing occurs at the beginning and end of every row. Details of the stitches and their written instructions below show how each of the situations would be worked.

Details of the stitches

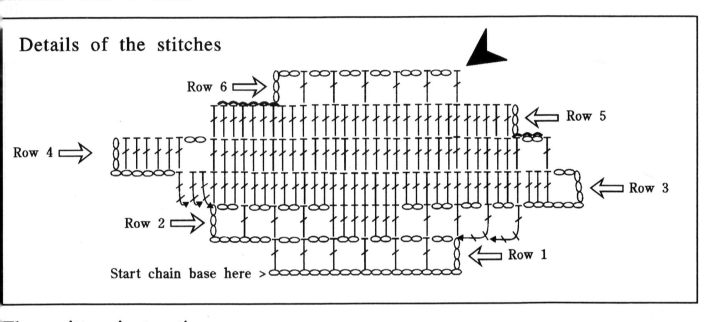

The written instructions

Refer to the abbreviations on page 4.
To start, make 24ch (19ch are the base line and 5ch are the turning ch for the first space of Row 1).
Row 1, 1tr into the 9th ch from the hook, (2ch, miss 2ch on the base line, 1tr into the next ch) 5 times, 11ch, turn.
Row 2, 1tr into 9th ch from the hook, (2ch, 1tr into the next tr) 3 times, (2tr over the next 2ch, 1tr into the next tr) twice, 2ch, 1tr into the next tr, 2ch, 1tr into two loops of the the 3rd of the 5 turning chain at the beginning of Row 1, 2ch, 1trtr into the same place as the last tr, 2ch, 1trtr under two loops of the middle notch of the last trtr, 11ch, turn.
Row 3, 1tr into the 9th ch from the hook, (1tr into the next ch) twice, (1tr onto the next trtr, 2tr over the next 2ch) twice, (1tr on the next tr, 2tr over the next 2ch) twice, (1tr on the next tr) 7 times, (2tr over the next 2ch, 1tr in the next tr) 3 times, 2tr over the next 2ch, 1tr into the next ch (catching up two loops of that ch) 1dbltr into that same ch, (1dbltr into the lower notch of the previous dbltr) twice, 9ch, turn.
Row 4, 1tr into the 5th ch from the hook, (1tr into the next ch) 4 times, 1tr on the next dbltr, 2ch, (1tr on the next tr) 31 times, 2ch, miss 2tr, 1tr on the next tr, turn.
Row 5, missing the tr just worked, ss into the next 3 stitches, 3ch, (1tr into the next tr) 30 times, turn.
Row 6, missing the tr just worked, ss into the next 6 stitches, 5ch, miss 2tr, 1tr on the next tr, (2ch, miss 2tr, 1tr on the next tr) 5 times. Fasten off.

Sample pattern No.3
Filet crochet corner

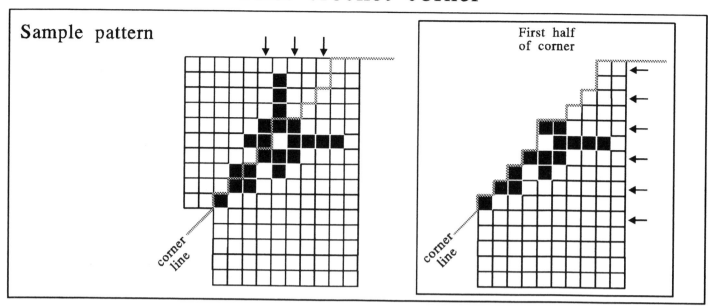

Sample pattern

First half of corner

corner line

corner line

In this book all the corners are marked with a corner line. The edging is completed into the first half of the corner, treating the corner line as a shaped edge.

A second chart isolates the first half of the corner with arrows showing which way the rows will be worked if the recommended start line is used.

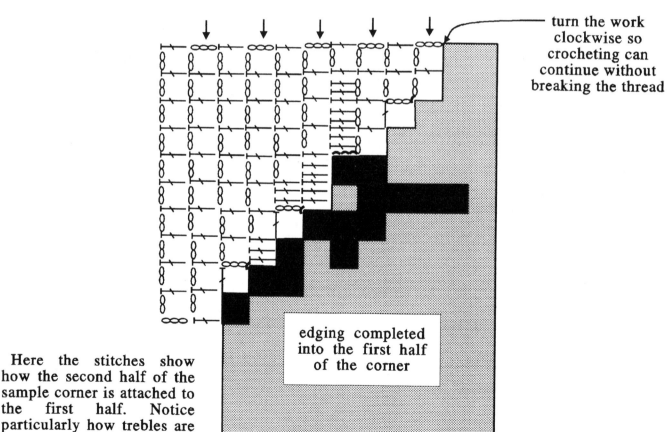

turn the work clockwise so crocheting can continue without breaking the thread

edging completed into the first half of the corner

Here the stitches show how the second half of the sample corner is attached to the first half. Notice particularly how trebles are used instead of chains and vice versa and also how slip stitches are used to get to the right position for another row.

10

ΦΦΦΦΦΦΦ SECTION ONE ΦΦΦΦΦΦΦ
Narrow edgings

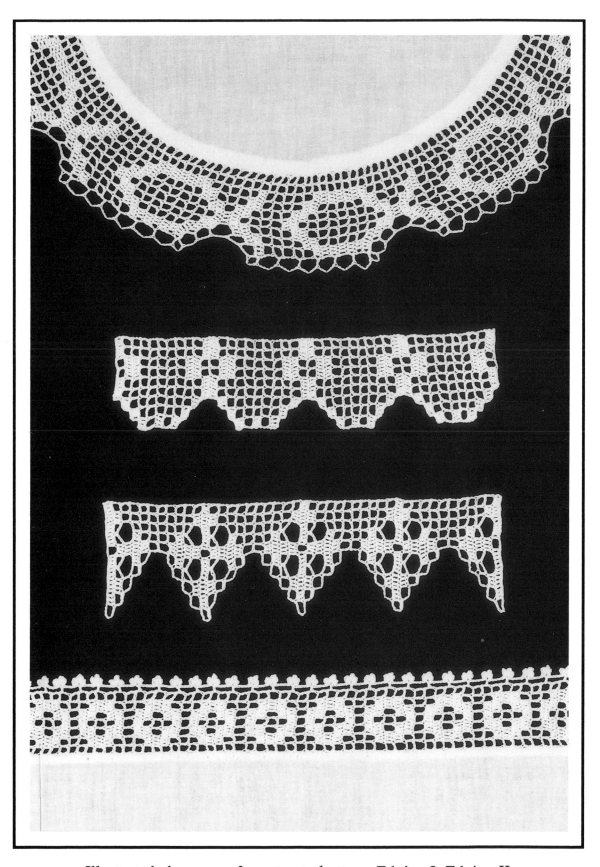

Illustrated above are, from top to bottom, Edging I, Edging II,
Edging III and Edging IV.
The patterns for these are on pages 13 and 14.

Uses for narrow edgings

.....on a rectangle of cloth.

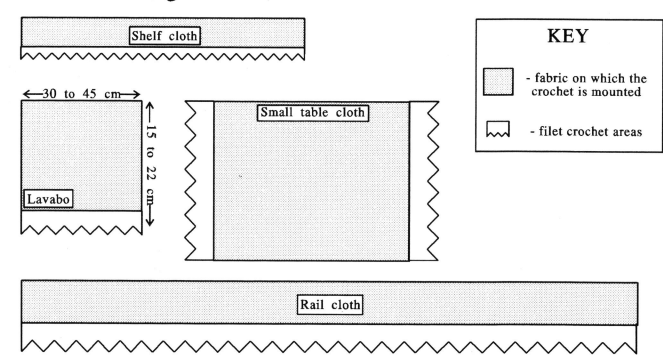

KEY

- fabric on which the crochet is mounted

- filet crochet areas

Shelf cloth

←30 to 45 cm→

15 to 22 cm

Lavabo

Small table cloth

Rail cloth

.....on a circle of cloth

A narrow edging up to 10 meshes deep can be made to curve as well as be straight.

Such an edging can be eased onto a circle of cloth from 12 inches in diameter as illustrated with Edging I in the photograph on page 11. Hem the circle of fabric first (this becomes easier the larger the circle). Circular cloths, of various sizes up to 60 inches in diameter, can be bought in linen shops.

Attach the completed edging before it is washed. The outer edge of the crochet which is not lying flat can then be made to do so when the completed mat is laundered and pinned out (see blocking and pinning on page 47).

Cloth for table or plinth

.....on clothing

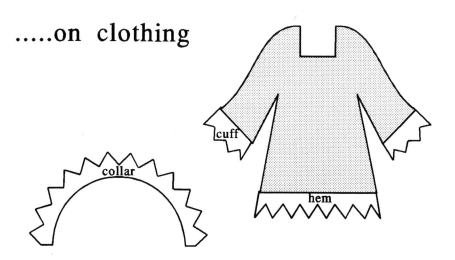

collar

cuff

hem

Attach a crochet edging to hemmed material with a whipping stitch, holding right sides together. Without stretching the crochet keep it in place with pins until it has been sewn so that the ends are aligned.

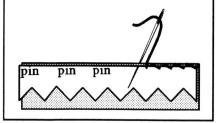

pin   pin   pin

EDGING I

Pattern repeats every 18 rows

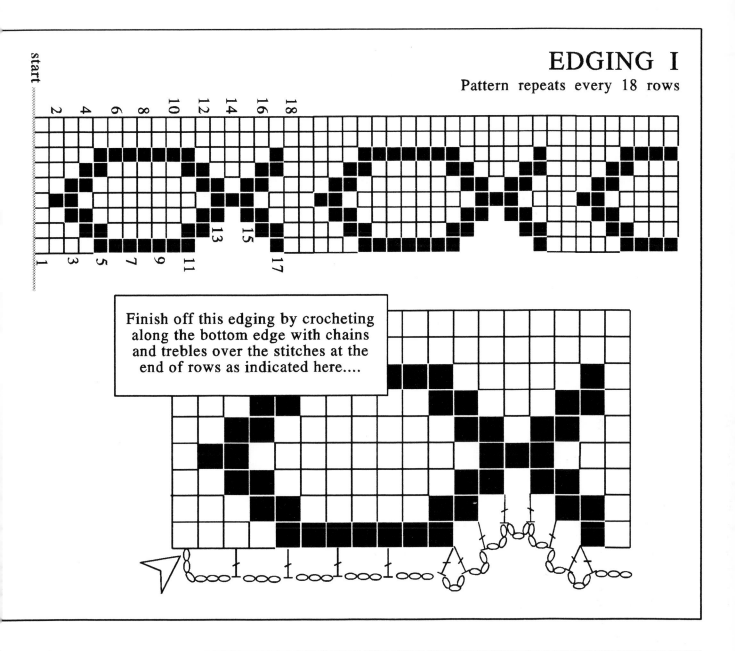

start

Finish off this edging by crocheting along the bottom edge with chains and trebles over the stitches at the end of rows as indicated here....

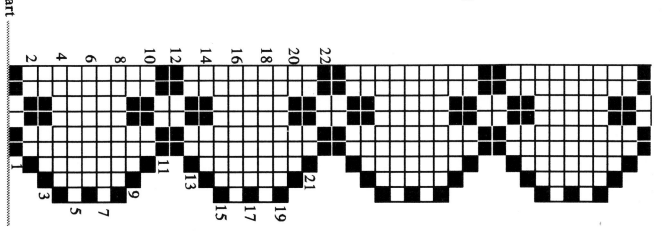

EDGING II

Pattern repeats every 11 rows.

22 rows are numbered because the second repeat is worked in the opposite direction to the first.

start

EDGING III

Pattern repeats every 11 rows

22 rows are numbered because the second repeat is worked in the opposite direction to the first.

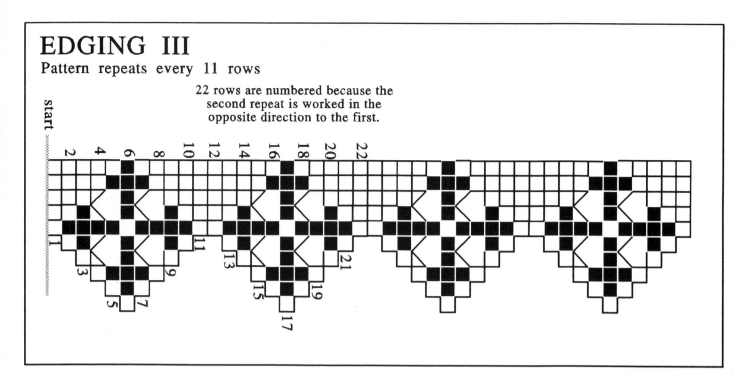

EDGING IV

Pattern repeats every 6 rows

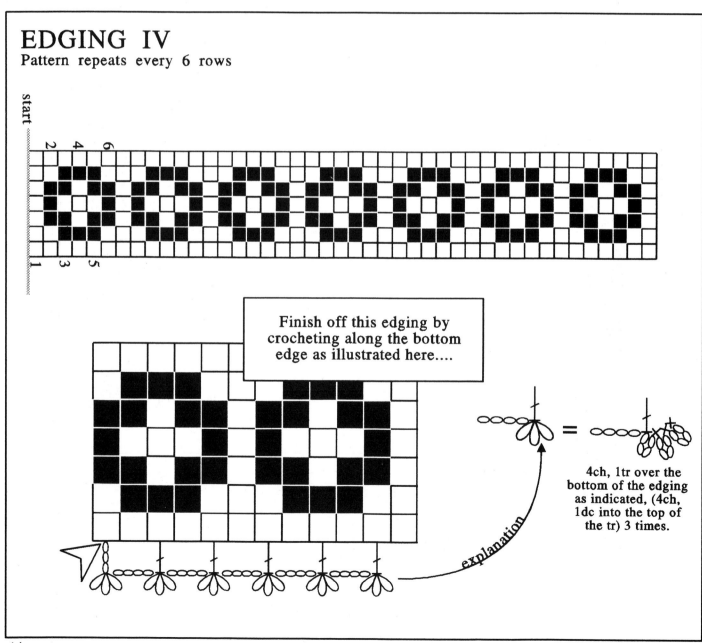

Finish off this edging by crocheting along the bottom edge as illustrated here....

4ch, 1tr over the bottom of the edging as indicated, (4ch, 1dc into the top of the tr) 3 times.

explanation

ΦΦΦΦΦΦΦ SECTION TWO ΦΦΦΦΦΦΦ
Deep edgings

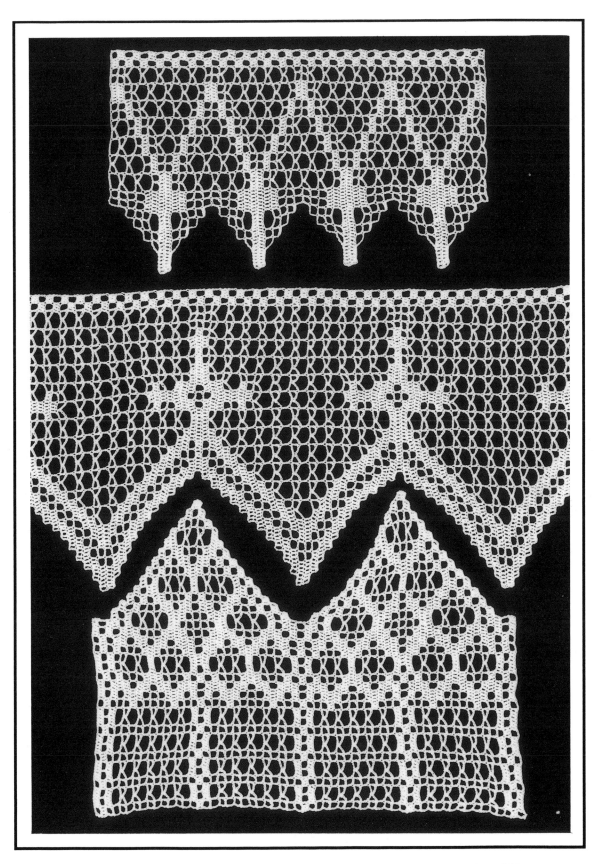

Illustrated above are, from top to bottom, Edging V, Edging VI
and Edging VII.
The patterns for these are on pages 17, 18 and 19.

Uses for deep edgings
.....on large rectangles of cloth

In addition to the ideas here, deep edgings can be used as shown for narrow edgings, except that deep edgings will not curve and they are heavier.

If the crochet is going to be hanging over an edge, make sure it is attached to enough weight of material to act as a counterbalance.

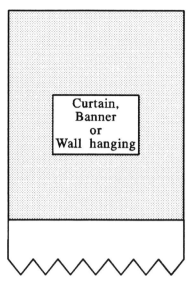

Curtain,
Banner
or
Wall hanging

KEY

- fabric on which the crochet is mounted

- filet crochet areas

.....on an Altar Cloth

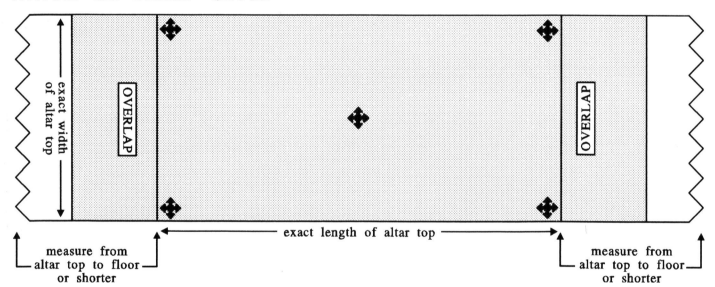

exact width of altar top

OVERLAP

OVERLAP

exact length of altar top

measure from altar top to floor or shorter

measure from altar top to floor or shorter

.....on an Altar Frontal

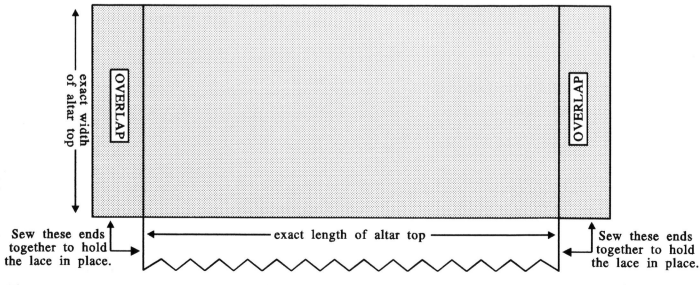

exact width of altar top

OVERLAP

OVERLAP

exact length of altar top

Sew these ends together to hold the lace in place.

Sew these ends together to hold the lace in place.

16

Pattern repeats every 12 rows

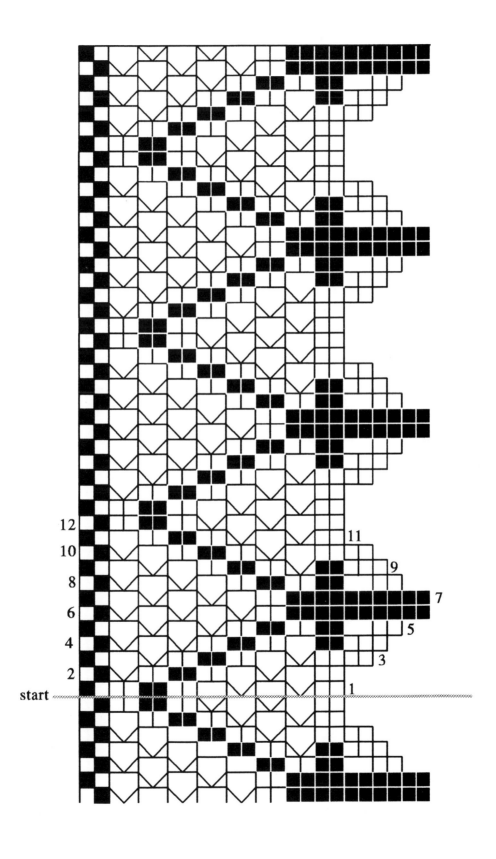

EDGING VI
Pattern repeats every 25 rows

50 rows are numbered because the second repeat is worked in the opposite direction to the first.

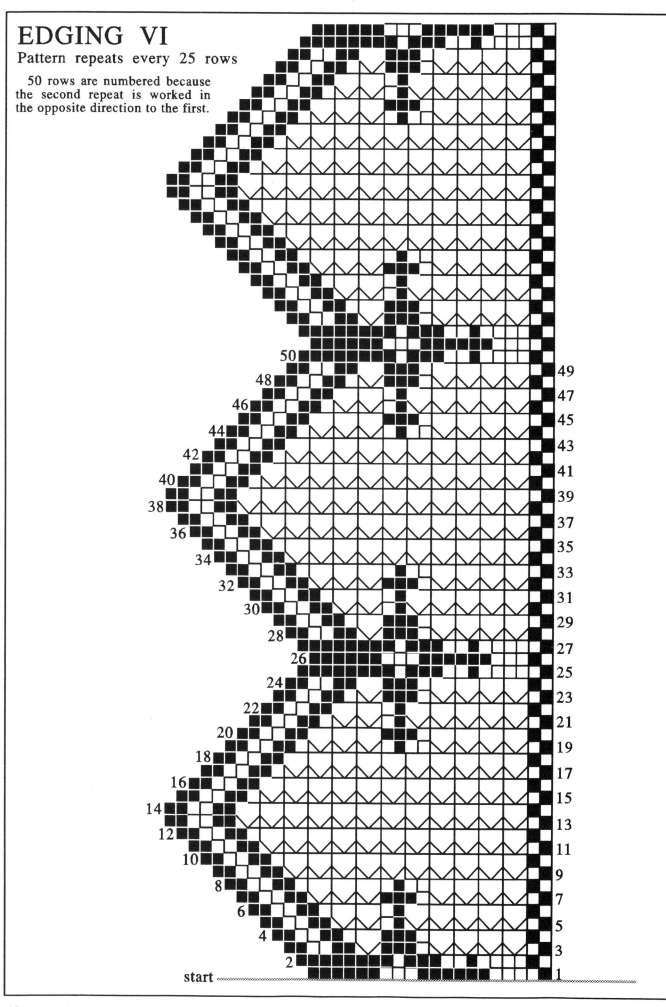

start

EDGING VII

Pattern repeats every 28 rows

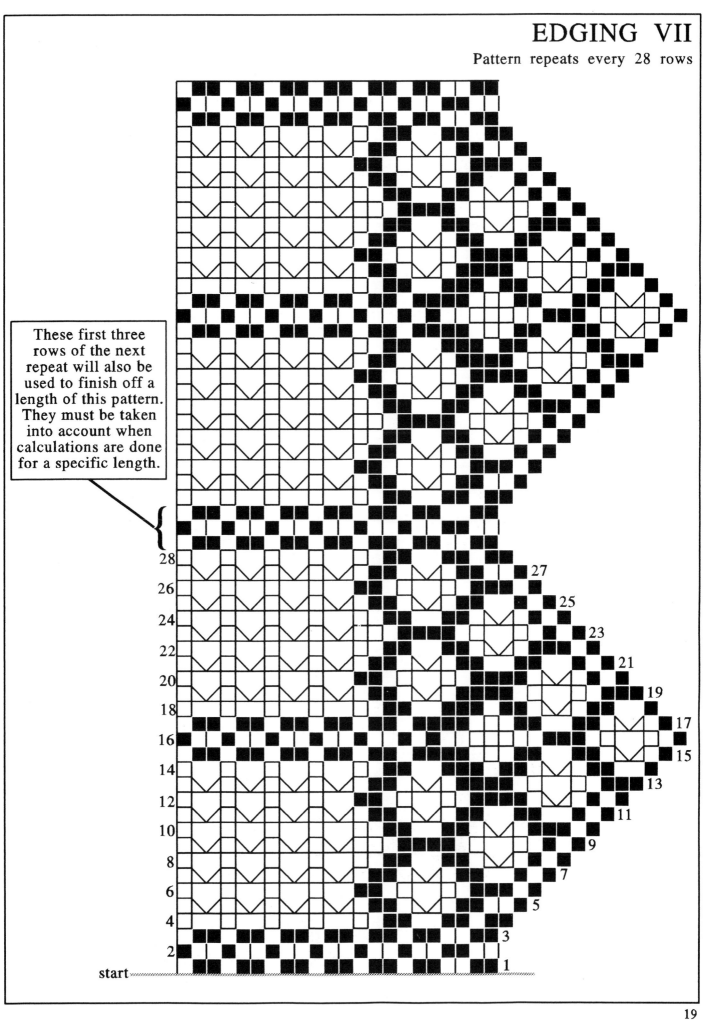

These first three rows of the next repeat will also be used to finish off a length of this pattern. They must be taken into account when calculations are done for a specific length.

start

EDGING VIII

Pattern repeats
every 24 rows

For a length of this
edging complete the last
repeat to row 24 then
finish off with row 1.

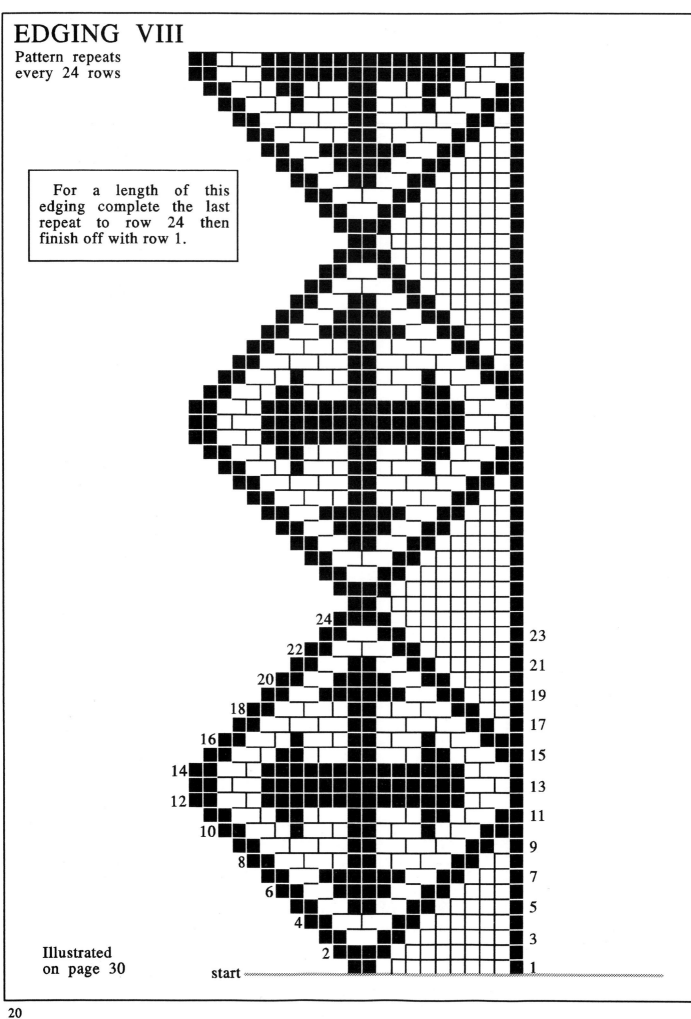

start

Illustrated
on page 30

ΦΦΦΦΦΦΦ SECTION THREE ΦΦΦΦΦΦΦ
Edgings with corners

Illustrated above are, from top to bottom, Edging X, Edging IX
and Edging XI.
The patterns for these are on pages 23, 24, 25 and 26.

Uses for edges with corners

.....on any size square or rectangular piece of cloth.

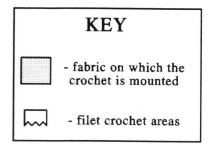

KEY

- fabric on which the crochet is mounted

- filet crochet areas

Make a table-cloth to be used not only in church, but also in the church hall, christian shop, home or school where appropriate.

Ready made cloths can be bought from linen shops or from suppliers of church linen.

Edgings with corners require more planning to ensure that the correct number of repeats of the chosen pattern are worked between each corner. First pin the finished crochet to the corners of the prepared fabric, then pin the sides in place. It is better to make the crochet slightly too big for the cloth, as the excess can be eased in with the whipping stitch (see page 12). If the edging is stretched because it was made too small, the cloth will not lie flat.

The square can be any size from a handkerchief to a large table-cloth, the difference is the thickness of crochet thread and the material on which it is mounted. Only the finest threads are suitable to crochet for handkerchiefs. The thicker threads are used for the larger items and the finished crochet must then be mounted on material of a corresponding thickness.

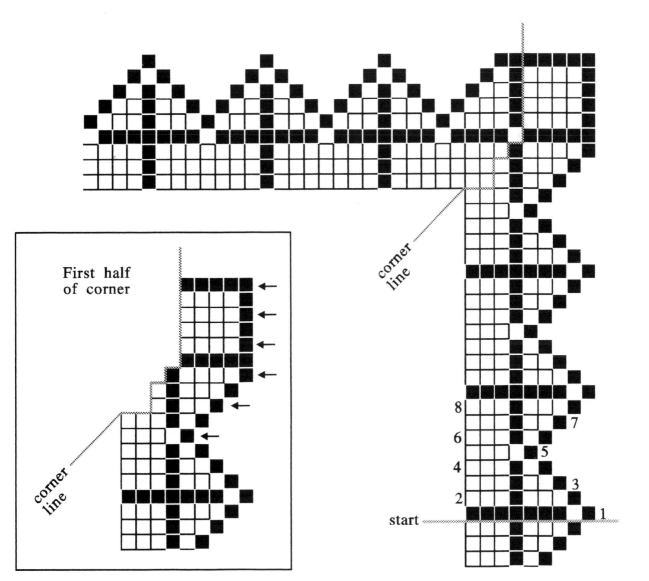

First half
of corner

corner
line

corner
line

8
7
6
5
4
3
2
1
start

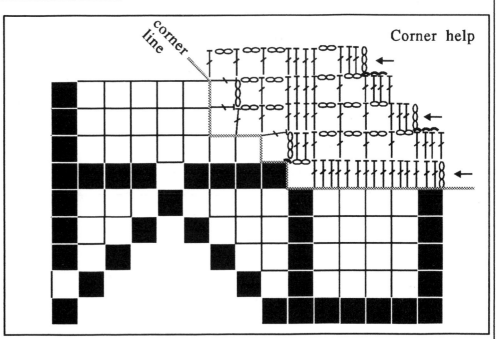

corner
line

Corner help

EDGING X

Pattern repeats every 6 rows
on the straight

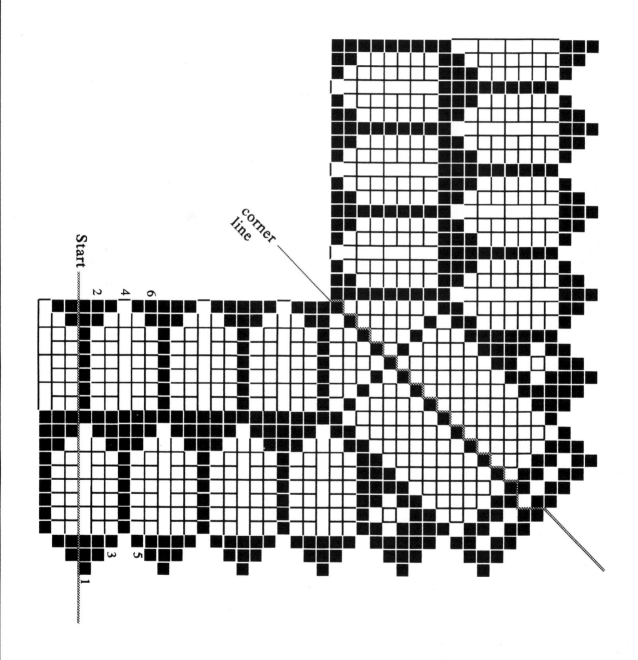

Edging X continued

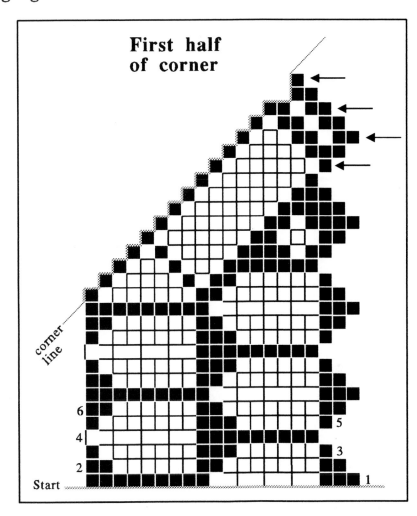

First half of corner

corner line

Start

1 2 3 4 5 6

corner line

Corner help

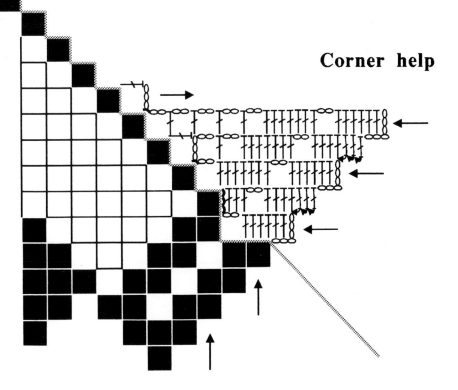

The stitches shown here help you to get started on the second half of this corner. All the other rows of the corner are joined in a similar manner. Notice that the first row of the following side overlaps the corner by one mesh. Ss into position here.

EDGING XI

Pattern repeats every 14 rows on the straight.

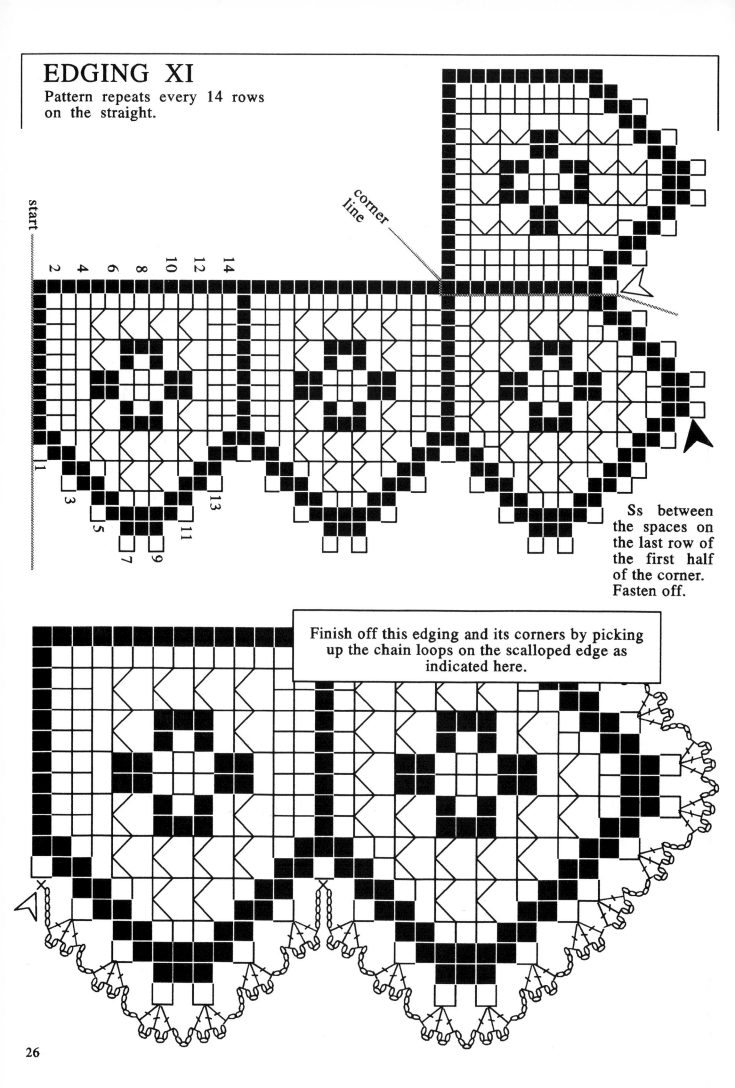

corner line

start

2 4 6 8 10 12 14

1 3 5 7 9 11 13

Ss between the spaces on the last row of the first half of the corner. Fasten off.

Finish off this edging and its corners by picking up the chain loops on the scalloped edge as indicated here.

ΦΦΦΦΦΦΦ SECTION FOUR ΦΦΦΦΦΦΦ
All corners

The sample for this illustration was worked by Mrs Iris Sabec.
She used a 1.25 hook with Coats Opera No.20 and the finished
measurement is 60cm across the longest diagonal.
It can be used as either a chalice cover or a mat.

The pattern details for the above are on pages 28 and 29 and
should only be attempted by an experienced worker who has
already followed other charts.

ALL CORNERS

As the title suggests, the making of this piece involves a continuous working of corners. Look at the pattern on this page to identify the start line and the four corner lines (they all converge on a central spot). Start from the centre. On the page opposite more details are given for the first segment from the start line to the first corner. The diagram underneath it gives corner help and should be used in conjunction with the full pattern on this page. Be careful not to lose your place in the centre and keep a constant check on the direction of your work.

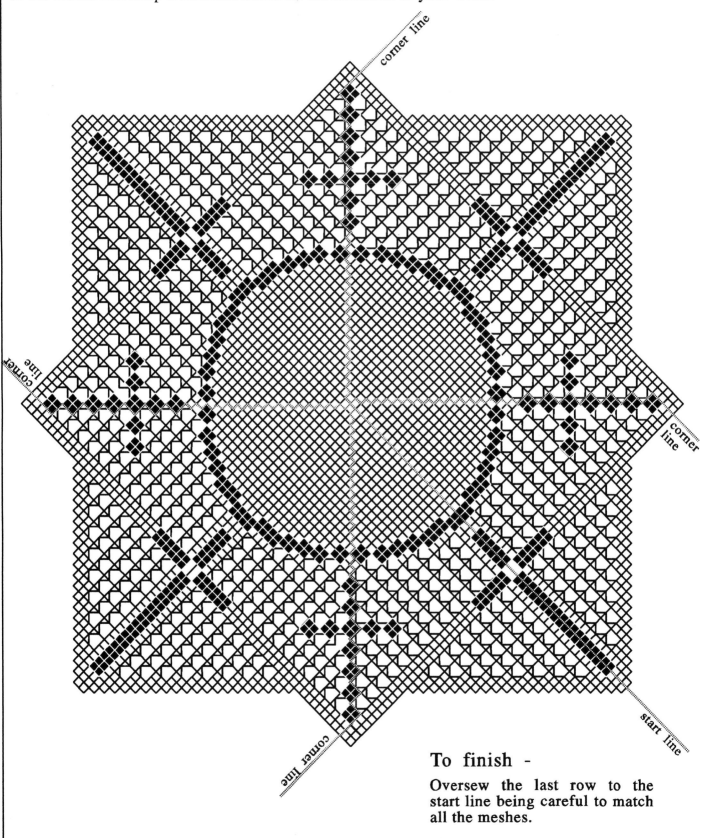

To finish -

Oversew the last row to the start line being careful to match all the meshes.

Starting segment

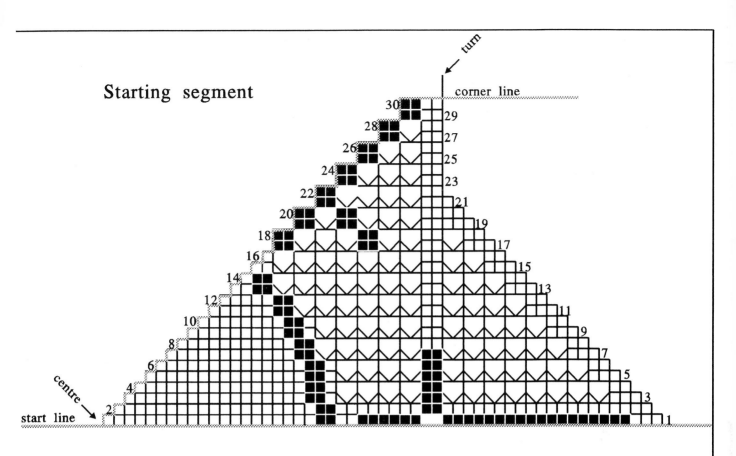

Corner help

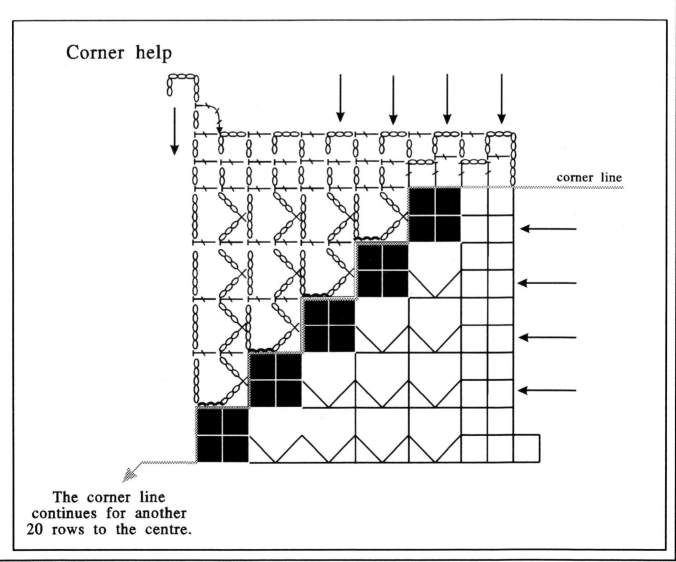

The corner line
continues for another
20 rows to the centre.

ΦΦΦΦΦΦ SECTION FIVE ΦΦΦΦΦΦ
Custom made ....

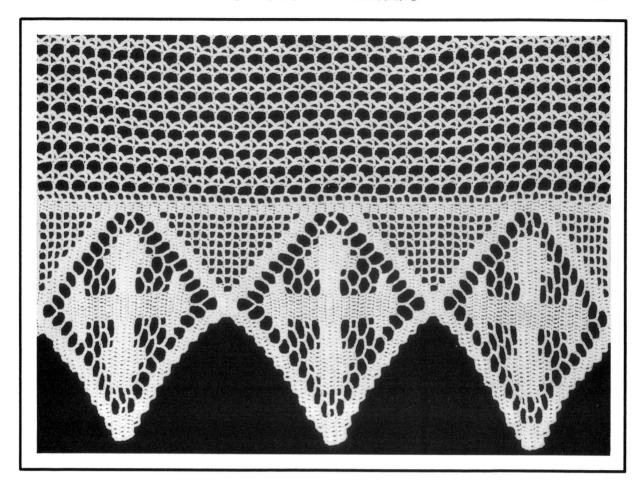

This illustration uses Edging VIII (page 20) but any edging could be used.

To make a curtain:

1) Choose an edging and make it as long as the width of the window or area to be covered.

2) If the edging doesn't finish at its straight side, ss along to that side.

3) With 5 turning chain, work a space over every row end on the straight side of your edging.

4) Count these spaces. An even number is needed for the bars and lacets. If there is an even number, continue the subsequent rows of bars and lacets in the usual way (Fig.1). For an odd number of rows, work the first row of bars into alternate spaces (Fig.2).

5) Continue to work alternate rows of bars and lacets for the desired length.

Fig.1   Fig.2

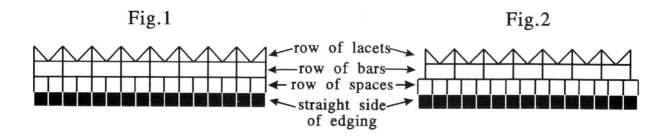

← row of lacets →
← row of bars →
← row of spaces →
← straight side →
of edging

ΦΦΦΦΦΦ SECTION FIVE ΦΦΦΦΦΦ
.... and combined patterns

Illustrated here is the end section of the Altar frontal made by Mrs Ellen Tierney for Our Lady's altar in Our Lady of the Angels Church, Nuneaton. The whole piece is illustrated on page 33.

In the illustration above three strips of filet crochet have been sewn together to form a very deep edging. Two advantages of this method are, firstly, that there is plenty of scope for originality and, secondly, mistakes are much quicker to rectify than if the piece had been worked all in one.

Over the next eight pages instructions, patterns and advice are given to encourage the adventurous crocheter to create their own individual piece, either large or small.

To make and assemble an edging with specially chosen wording.

 Make a tension square

...using your chosen hook and thread work 22 rows of 22 spaces.

This tension sample will give a good idea of how many squares of the patterns will be worked to the inch in both directions.

There is no need for the worker to change their personal tension. As long as the same person crochets a complete item everything will be in proportion.

 Measure the area

The initial preparation is very important.

If the finished lace is to go in a specific place, take all the measurements, width, height, breadth etc., of the area to be covered.

For the altar frontal shown opposite, and illustrated in detail on page 31, Mrs Tierney used a 1.25 hook with No.20 crochet cotton. When finished it measured seven feet long and one foot deep. It does not obscure the monogram in the stonework underneath.

Another practical point to remember is the weight of a lace overhang. Is there room on the supporting ledge for enough material to hold it in place?

 Choose the wording

The patterns for the letters are on pages 34 to 38. They are worked from left to right so all the wording will be worked as it is written. Notice that the letters are differing widths, e.g. an I is narrower than an M. At the top of page 34 is a spacer which is put between, before and after words.

 Work the words

The strip of words is worked first, then other edgings can be planned to accompany the result.

If your preparation has been thorough the crocheted words should be the length you require. Don't worry if they are one or two inches too long as this can disappear if the work is not stretched out too much when laundered and mounted. If the wording is too short then ends can be added to the final lace (see '8' opposite).

 Make a bottom edging

Choose any edging and calculate where to start so both ends will match. The word PEACE below, with a spacer either side of it, covers 96 rows. One repeat of the edging chosen here covers 11 rows. 96 divided by 11 gives 8 remainder 8. This remaindered 8 is divided in half for the two ends. So you will see that there are 8 full repeats of the edging pattern with 4 rows of the repeat at each end.

The words and the edging will be sewn together.

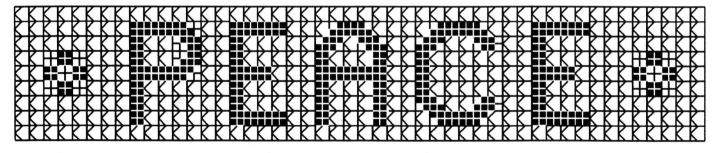

6 Make a top edging

If you decide to use Edging XII (page 38) or Edging XV (page 42) then there is also a top edging to match for each of them. Of the two designs the butterfly edging is the easiest to calculate. It is worked from the centre out in both directions so you just need to find the centre of your wording strip and count the rows out to the end.

 8 Add ends if required

The assembled edging can be lengthened by crocheting onto both ends following the pattern on page 39.

 7 Sew together the crocheted strips

As the letters of the alphabet (patterns on pages 34 to 37) are surrounded by bars and lacets the crocheted words will probably stretch out more than the edging which has been made to match. Before sewing together put ties in every 10 rows to temporarily conect the strips in the right position (see the diagram below).

Sit up to a table and have the crochet flat. Oversew the joins on the wrong side making one stitch to each row end, not too tightly (see also page 39).

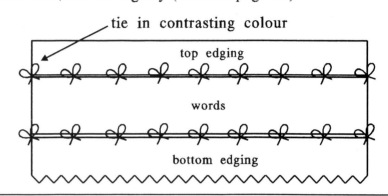

tie in contrasting colour

top edging

words

bottom edging

 9 Illustrated above is the finished project. Made by Mrs Ellen Tierney, as mentioned on pages 31 and 32, it used up 4 x 50gm balls of Coats Opera No.20.

The Alphabet - pages 34 to 37

Start each letter's pattern along its left side edge. The row numbers are not marked as it would be confusing when words were being worked.

The total number of rows is shown with each letter to help your calculations.

A = 14 rows

B = 14 rows

C = 16 rows

D = 14 rows

E = 12 rows

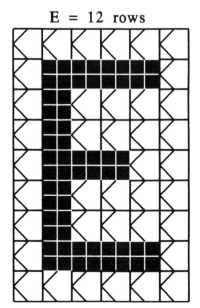

F = 12 rows

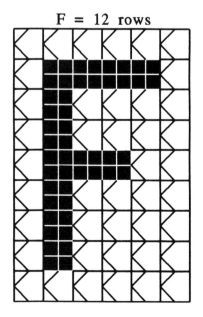

G = 16 rows

H = 14 rows

I = 10 rows

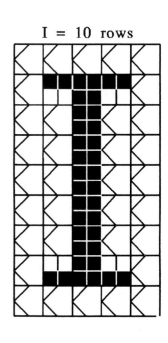

J = 14 rows

K = 14 rows

L = 12 rows

M = 16 rows

N = 14 rows

O = 16 rows

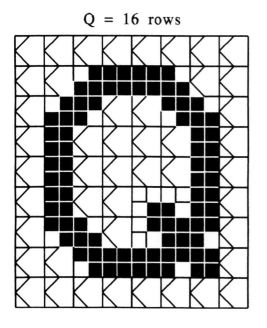

P = 14 rows

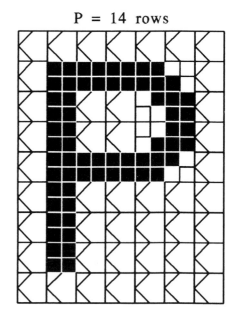

Q = 16 rows

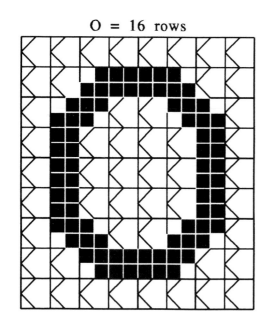

R = 14 rows

S = 14 rows

T = 14 rows

U = 14 rows

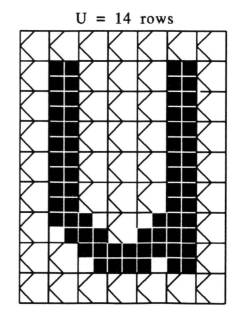

V = 14 rows

W = 16 rows

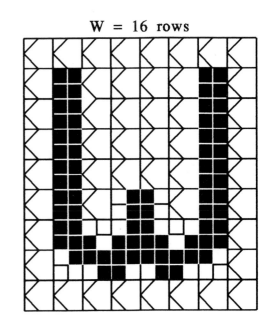

X = 14 rows

Y = 16 rows

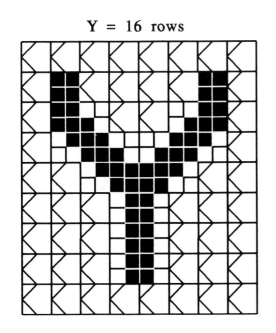

Z = 12 rows

37

EDGING XII with matching top
Pattern repeats every 12 rows.

Make them match

You may have calculated the need to start these edgings in the middle of a repeat. If so, remember to start them both in the same place!

ENDS

The sketch on the left shows both ends in place.

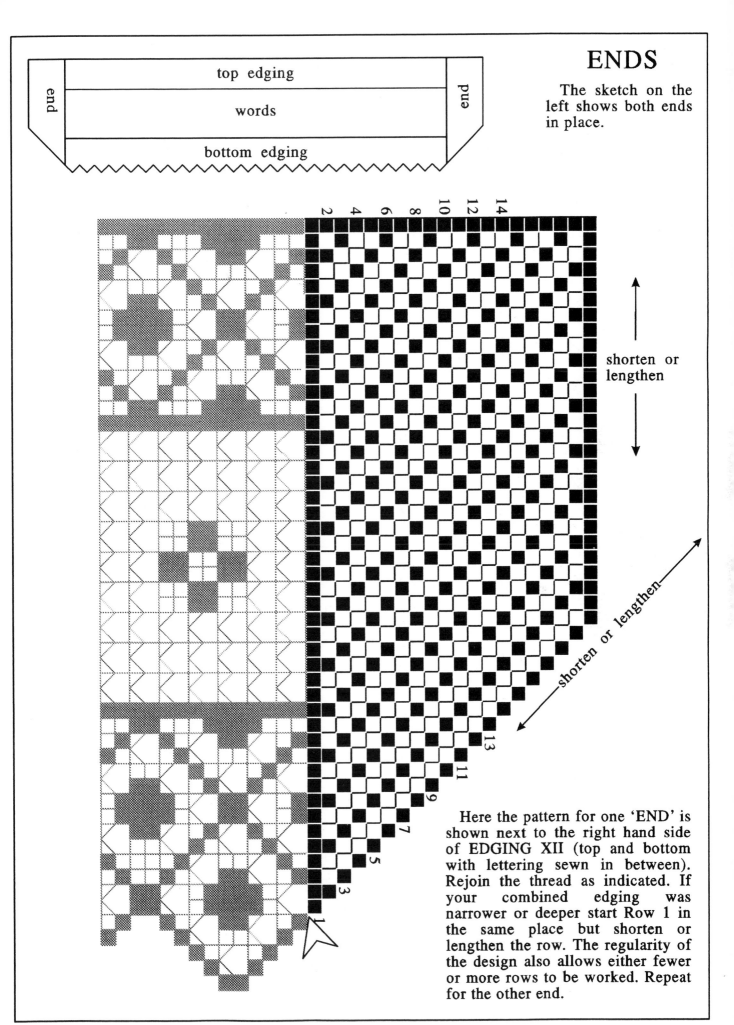

shorten or lengthen

shorten or lengthen

Here the pattern for one 'END' is shown next to the right hand side of EDGING XII (top and bottom with lettering sewn in between). Rejoin the thread as indicated. If your combined edging was narrower or deeper start Row 1 in the same place but shorten or lengthen the row. The regularity of the design also allows either fewer or more rows to be worked. Repeat for the other end.

ΦΦΦΦΦΦΦ SECTION SIX ΦΦΦΦΦΦΦ
Other edgings

Illustrated on the left above is Edging XV then, on the right from
top to bottom, are Edging XIII, Edging XIV and Edging XVI.
The patterns for these are on pages 41 and 42.

EDGING XIII

Pattern repeats every 9 rows

18 rows are numbered because the
second repeat is worked in the
opposite direction to the first.

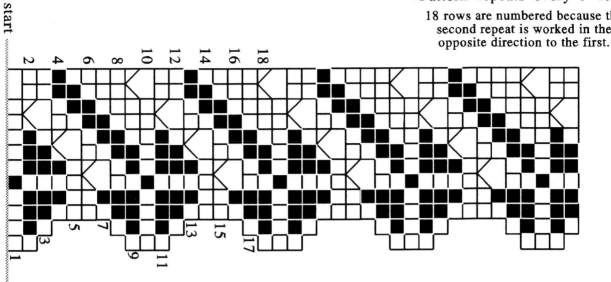

EDGING XIV

Pattern repeats every 16 rows

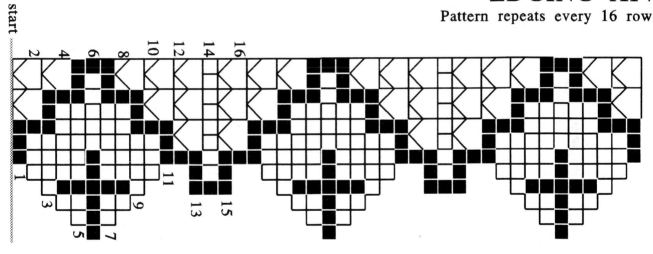

Beads are added to this edging, drooping from each point. Count the number of points to your edging and thread that number of beads onto your ball before rejoining it in the appropriate place. There are 5ch in all the chain loops and they are attached to the edging as shown below with a dc. Where a bead is shown, pass it up from the ball and hold it in place with the next stitch.

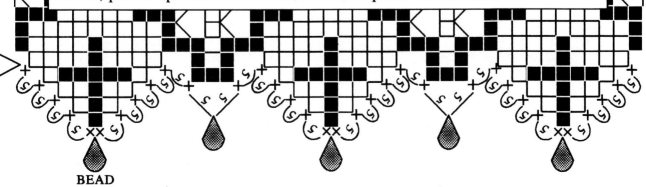

BEAD

EDGING XV (right half)

With matching top (see page 48).

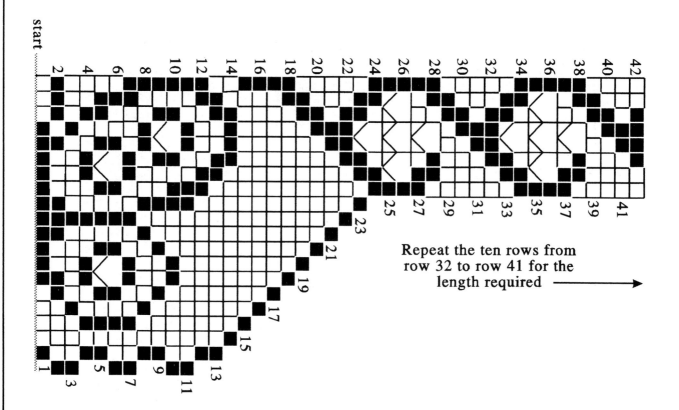

Repeat the ten rows from
row 32 to row 41 for the
length required ———→

This edging is worked in two halves. The start line of chain will be used twice and it
is easiest to pick up one thread of these chains the first time and the other two threads
the second time. Complete the first half from the pattern above. For the second half
(see page 48), rejoin the thread on the other side of the start line, at the shaped edge as
before.

EDGING XVI

Pattern repeats every 12 rows

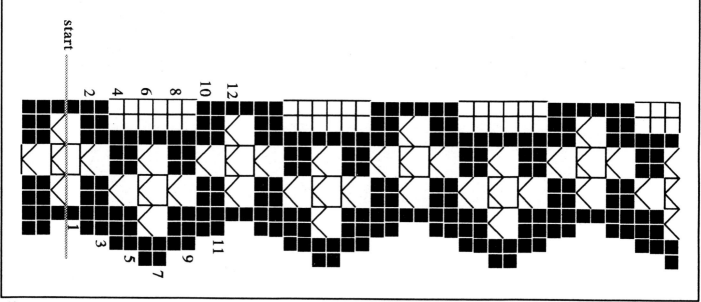

ΦΦΦΦΦΦΦ SECTION SEVEN ΦΦΦΦΦΦΦ
Bookmarks

Illustrated on the left above is Bookmark I and on the right Bookmark II.
The patterns for these are on pages 44 and 45 respectively.

BOOKMARK I

This pattern is worked in two
  halves from the centre out.

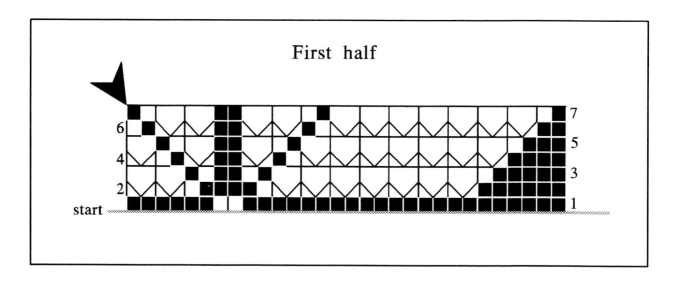

First half

7
6
5
4
3
2
start
1

Second half

When the first half is finished
turn the work over and rejoin the
thread as indicated for the
second half. The start line is
used twice as with EDGING XV.
So, where the chains of the start
line are worked, it is easiest to
pick up one thread the first time
and two threads the second
time.

BOOKMARK I can be used on
its own or mounted on ribbon. It
can be put on some coloured felt
and slipped inside a plastic
bookmark cover. It could also be
put into a card with a rectangular
pre-cut aperture.

BOOKMARK II

This pattern is worked in three rounds.

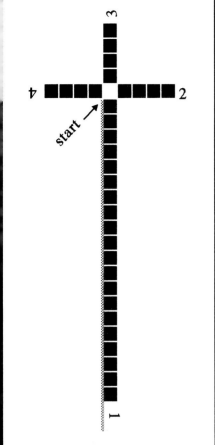

Round one

Start the base chain from the centre of the cross down the long arm as indicated. Row 1 is the 20 blocks back to the centre. Make the base and turning chain for Row 2 and work the 4 blocks back to the centre. For Rows 3 and 4, repeat Row 2. Slip stitch to the start point.

Round two

Slip stitch along the bottom of the last block of Row 1 in the first round. 5ch, miss 2ch, 1tr into the next ch (this space is outlined). Continue making the spaces all round the cross going down and up all four arms. Place 1tr, 5ch, 1tr on the outer corners of the arms. Between the arms work 2tr together putting one at the end of one arm and the other at the beginning of the next.

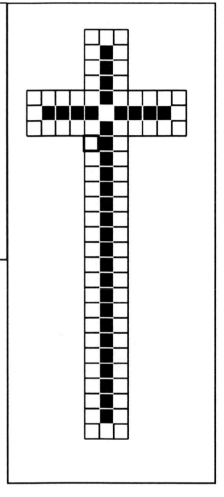

Round three

Slip stitch into the 3rd of 5ch at the beginning of the second round and ss on over the next 3 stitches. Complete this round in the same way as round two.

BOOKMARK II can be used on its own or could be mounted on a veil or other material. It could also be put into a card with a rectangular or oval pre-cut aperture.

Adapt edgings to make bookmarks

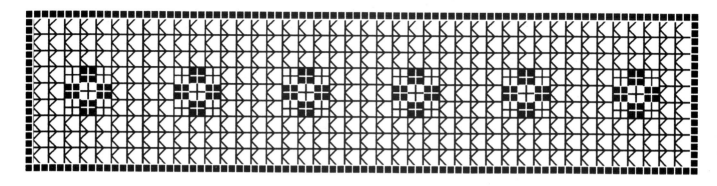

Take letters of the alphabet (pages 34 to 37) or, as here, just spacers, and add a border of blocks. As it is quite wide this design would be best worked in a fine thread.

Take Edging IV and finish it off all round with the trebles and chain loops explained on page 14.

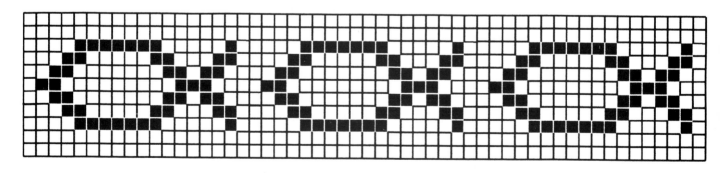

Here Edging I has been adapted so that all its sides are straight. Finish off in a contrasting colour, working 2dc into each space and a dc into the tr between, all the way round the outside. A section like this can be taken from any design.

Blocking and pinning

Pinning out the finished crochet work is a time-consuming process compared with pressing and ironing it, but it is well worth all the effort.

On completing an item rinse it out in warm water, with soap if required. This will draw in all the stitches, making them even and most unwanted loopiness will disappear.

The work can then be pinned out and left to dry. It will then look exactly as you have set it with the pins.

1) If this was the pattern....

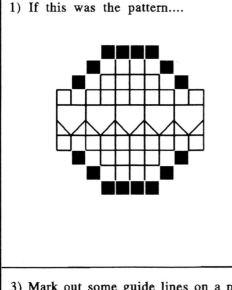

2) the finished work would look something like this....

3) Mark out some guide lines on a piece of plain material and lay it on the pinning-out surface such as a cork or polystyrene board.

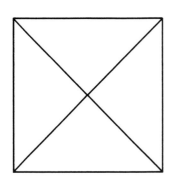

4) Always put the pins under at least two loops of thread if not a whole treble or row of chains. Angle the pins out to take the strain.

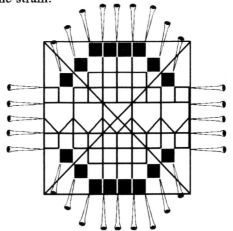

Large pieces

Spread a large table-cloth or sheet on an area of carpet in a warm room which will not be used for a few hours. With a vast supply of pins, carefully pin the crochet out to the size required. When the crochet is dry, remove all the pins and be sure not to leave any lying around!

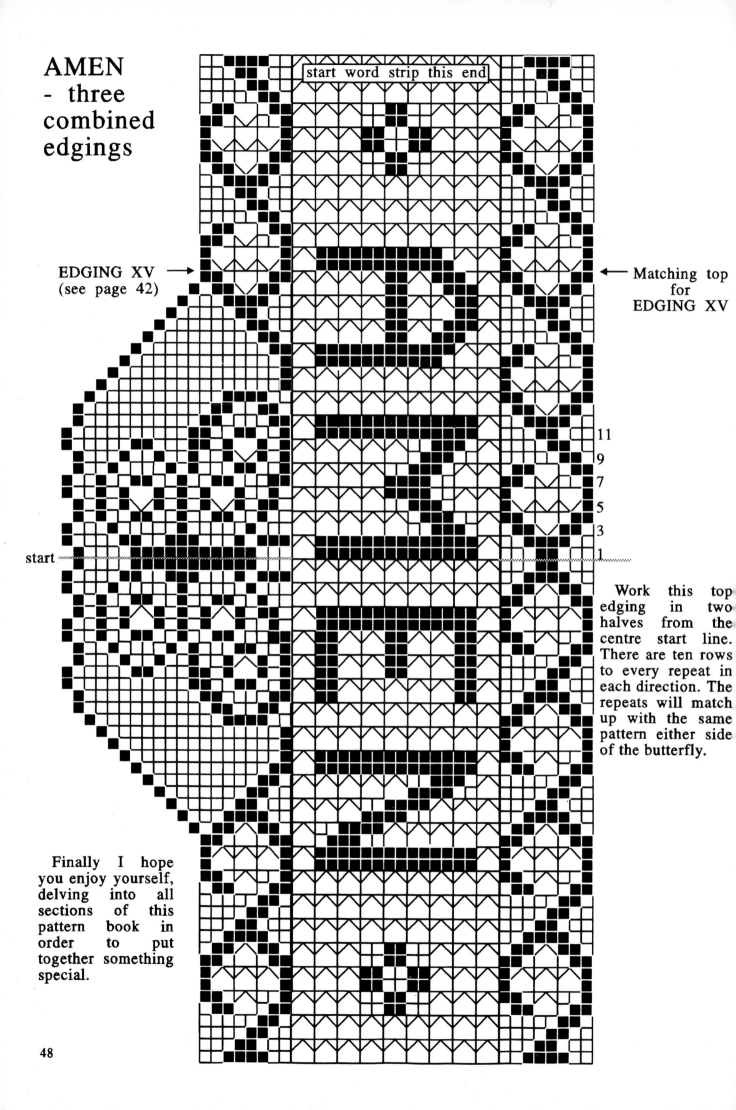

AMEN
- three combined edgings

EDGING XV → (see page 42)

Matching top for EDGING XV ←

start word strip this end

11
9
7
5
3
start 1

Work this top edging in two halves from the centre start line. There are ten rows to every repeat in each direction. The repeats will match up with the same pattern either side of the butterfly.

Finally I hope you enjoy yourself, delving into all sections of this pattern book in order to put together something special.

start word strip this end